Guelph

J951.95 DAN
Daniels-Cowart, Catrina, author.
South Korea

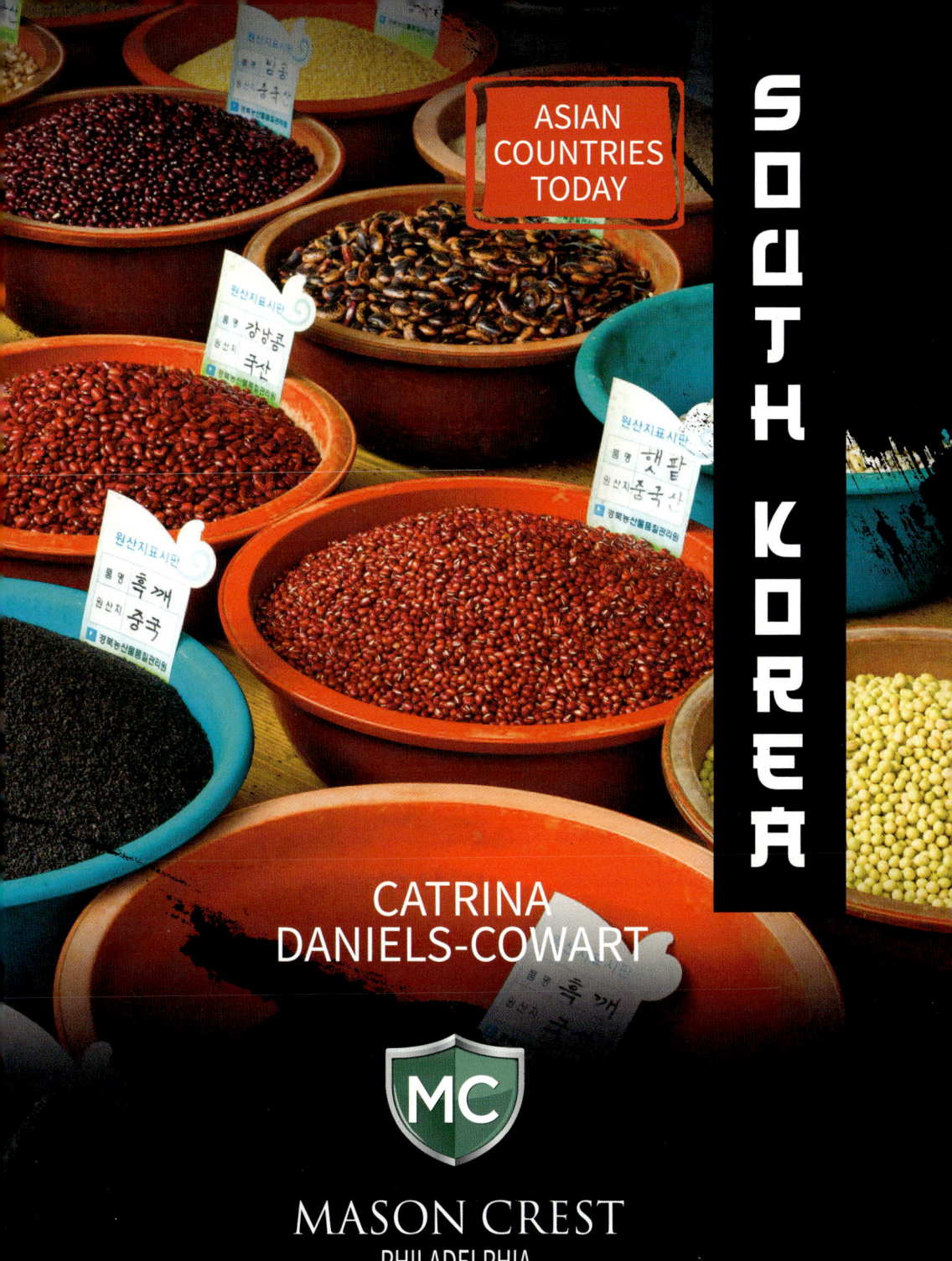

ASIAN COUNTRIES TODAY

SOUTH KOREA

CATRINA DANIELS-COWART

MC

MASON CREST
PHILADELPHIA
MIAMI

MASON CREST

450 Parkway Drive, Suite D, Broomall, Pennsylvania 19008
(866) MCP-BOOK (toll-free) • www.masoncrest.com

Copyright © 2020 by Mason Crest, an imprint of National Highlights, Inc. All rights reserved. No part of this publication may be reproduced or transmitted in any form or by any means, electronic or mechanical, including photocopying, recording, taping, or any information storage and retrieval system, without permission in writing from the publisher.

Printed in the United States of America

First printing
9 8 7 6 5 4 3 2 1

ISBN (hardback) 978-1-4222-4267-4
ISBN (series) 978-1-4222-4263-6
ISBN (ebook) 978-1-4222-7553-5

Cataloging-in-Publication Data on file with the Library of Congress

Developed and Produced by National Highlights Inc.
Editor: Susan Uttendorfsky
Interior and cover design: Jana Rade
Production: Michelle Luke

QR CODES AND LINKS TO THIRD-PARTY CONTENT

You may gain access to certain third-party content ("Third-Party Sites") by scanning and using the QR Codes that appear in this publication (the "QR Codes"). We do not operate or control in any respect any information, products, or services on such Third-Party Sites linked to by us via the QR Codes included in this publication, and we assume no responsibility for any materials you may access using the QR Codes. Your use of the QR Codes may be subject to terms, limitations, or restrictions set forth in the applicable terms of use or otherwise established by the owners of the Third-Party Sites. Our linking to such Third-Party Sites via the QR Codes does not imply an endorsement or sponsorship of such Third-Party Sites or the information, products, or services offered on or through the Third-Party Sites, nor does it imply an endorsement or sponsorship of this publication by the owners of such Third-Party Sites.

CONTENTS

South Korea at a Glance..6
Chapter 1: South Korea's Geography & Landscape................. 11
Chapter 2: The Government & History of South Korea............. 19
Chapter 3: The South Korean Economy..................................27
Chapter 4: Citizens of South Korea—
People, Customs & Culture 45
Chapter 5: Famous Cities of South Korea................................65
Chapter 6: A Bright Future for South Korea 77
South Korean Food 82
Festivals & Holidays..86
Series Glossary of Key Terms...88
Chronology..90
Further Reading & Internet Resources...91
Index..92
Organizations to Contact..95
Author's Biography & Credits...96

KEY ICONS TO LOOK FOR:

WORDS TO UNDERSTAND: These words with their easy-to-understand definitions will increase the reader's understanding of the text while building vocabulary skills.

SIDEBARS: This boxed material within the main text allows readers to build knowledge, gain insights, explore possibilities, and broaden their perspectives by weaving together additional information to provide realistic and holistic perspectives.

EDUCATIONAL VIDEOS: Readers can view videos by scanning our QR codes, providing them with additional educational content to supplement the text. Examples include news coverage, moments in history, speeches, iconic sports moments, and much more!

TEXT-DEPENDENT QUESTIONS: These questions send the reader back to the text for more careful attention to the evidence presented there.

RESEARCH PROJECTS: Readers are pointed toward areas of further inquiry connected to each chapter. Suggestions are provided for projects that encourage deeper research and analysis.

SERIES GLOSSARY OF KEY TERMS: This back-of-the-book glossary contains terminology used throughout this series. Words found here increase the reader's ability to read and comprehend higher-level books and articles in this field.

SOUTH KOREA AT A GLANCE

China

Myanmar
Laos
Thailand
Vietnam
Cambodia

Sri Lanka

Brunei
Malaysia
° Singapore

Indo

6 SOUTH KOREA

The Geography of South Korea

Location:
Eastern Asia, bordering the Sea of Japan and the Yellow Sea. It is located on the southern half of the Korean peninsula

Area: Approximately the size of Pennsylvania
total: 38,505 square miles (99,729 sq. km)
land: 37,421 square miles (96,920 sq. km)
water: 1,081 square miles (2,800 sq. km)

Borders: North Korea

Climate: A temperate climate with heavy rainfall in summer compared to the winter. Winters are cold

Terrain: Mostly hills and mountains; wide coastal plains in west and south

Elevation Extremes:
lowest point: Sea of Japan 0 feet (0 meters) at sea level

highest point: Hallasan 6,397.64 feet (1,950 m) (4,095 m) above sea level

Natural Hazards:
Flooding and high winds due to occasional typhoons, volcanism with low-level seismic activity in the southwest

Source: www.cia.gov 2017

FLAG OF SOUTH KOREA

The flag of South Korea is also known as *taegukki* in Korean. It was officially adopted in 1950 when the country divided into North and South Korea. The symbolism was developed in the nineteenth century, using a red and blue yin-and-yang in the middle of the flag and trigrams in each of the four corners. The four trigrams are based on Chinese philosophy and represent water, earth, fire, and sky. The flag's background is white, which represents hope, peace, and purity.

Interestingly, the lack of a flag representing Korea wasn't an issue until late into the Choson Dynasty. In 1876, it was determined that a flag would be needed because of the possible Japan-Korea Treaty of 1876. There were some flags created prior to this date, like the *taegukki* of the Choson Dynasty. It is a contrast against today's flag. It was red, black, orange, and white. From the start, the majority appeared to have a yin-yang-like symbol in the center, as well as symbolism for the elements.

The People of South Korea

Population: 51,418,097

Ethnic Groups: Homogeneous

Age Structure:
0–14 years: 13.03% (6,700,066)
15-24 years: 12.19% (6,266,253)
25-54 years: 45.13% (23,207,028)
55-64 years: 15.09% (7,760,827)
65 years and over: 14.55% (7,483,576)

Population Growth Rate:
0.44%

Death Rate:
6.3 deaths/1,000 pop.

Migration Rate:
2.5 migrant(s)/1,000 pop.

Infant Mortality Rate:
3 deaths/1,000 live births

Life Expectancy at Birth:
total population: 82.5 years
male: 79.4 years
female: 85.8 years

Total Fertility Rate:
1.27 children born/woman

Religions:
Protestant 19.7%, Buddhist 15.5%, Catholic 7.9%, none 56.9%, Confucianism is also widely practiced

Languages:
Korean, English

Literacy Rate:
97.9 % %

Source: www.cia.gov 2018

Deogyusan National Park is located in the provinces of Jeollabuk-do and Gyeongsangnam-do.

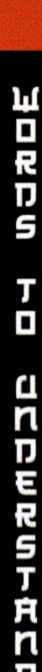

WORDS TO UNDERSTAND

demilitarized: an area from which all military personnel and equipment have been removed

peninsula: a piece of land that is almost entirely surrounded by water and is attached to a larger land area

strait: a narrow passage of water that connects two large areas of water

SOUTH KOREA'S GEOGRAPHY & LANDSCAPE

CHAPTER 1

South Korea is small but mighty, taking up a space that is slightly smaller than the state of Pennsylvania. Located in the southern half of the Korean **peninsula**, South Korea is located near China and North Korea, and Japan is across the Sea of Japan. South Korea shares one of the world's most heavily militarized borders with North Korea.

Geography

The country has maritime claims, including the Korea **Strait**. It also has mountainous, hilly terrain with wide coastal plains located in the south and western regions of the country. Approximately 3,004 square miles (7,790 square kilometers) are irrigated.

Around 70 percent of the country is mountainous, so the population tends to be found in lowland areas in dense cities. The capital, Seoul, is located in the Gyeonggi Province and contains the highest population of any part of the country. This is also where the busy port, Incheon, is. In the northeast of the country, Gangwon is the least populated area.

There are four regions in South Korea. The region in the east is a diverse area of high mountains and coastal plains. To the west are coastal plains, river basins, and hills. The southwest is mainly mountainous. Lastly, the southeastern region is where the broad basin of the Nakdong River is situated.

As much of South Korea is mountainous, it makes farming difficult, so much of its food has to be imported. In fact, only about a third of South Korea's land mass is lowland, and potentially suitable for agriculture.

About three thousand islands are situated off the western and southern coasts of South Korea. The largest island Jeju is 62 miles (100 kilometers) from the mainland. The island has an area of 712 square miles

Jeju Island

Jeju Island is a beautiful location off the coast of South Korea. The highest mountain in the nation is located there, and there are direct flights to the island from places such as Beijing, Osaka, and Shanghai. The visa requirements aren't strict, which also makes this a popular tourist destination.

Jeju Island is home to a UNESCO geopark known as the Manjang Cave. This natural wonder is over 5 miles (8 kilometers) long and was formed with cooled lava. It's just one aftereffect of the island's volcanic history. Visitors looking to experience the island's volcanic craters can head to Sunrise Peak, also known as Seongsan Ilchulbong. This is accessible by bridge, and there are many activities along the route. Visitors find that the tourist destination has parking and shopping, adding to the scenic beauty of the photo-worthy landmark.

(1,845 square kilometers). It is the location of the highest point in South Korea which is the extinct volcano of Hallasan. South Korea is a wonderful place to visit. It is a country of ancient buddhist temples, tea plantations, interesting neighborhoods, vibrant and fashionable cities, and stunningly beautiful islands. It's equally known for its lush countryside, with rolling hills dotted with cherry trees, and its fishing villages along the coastline.

The Climate

The nation's climate is temperate, and it's normal to see heavier rainfall throughout the summer months than in the winter. There is a risk of monsoons, which can lead to flooding and wind damage. South Korea has four seasons with long winters and

Jeju City on Jeju Island. The island is situated off the coast of South Korea.

SOUTH KOREA'S GEOGRAPHY & LANDSCAPE

short summers, falls, and springs. Temperature-wise, the mean temperature is around 23 degrees Fahrenheit (-5 degrees Celsius) in January, up to an average 75 degrees Fahrenheit (24 degrees Celsius) in July.

Each year there is at least 29 inches (75 centimeters) of rain; less than this is unusual. Normally rainfall exceeds 39 inches (100 centimeters), but it is also typical to see a drought around every eight years. Most years have typhoons, which impact the country in late summer through August. During typhoons, torrential rains add to the above measurements for yearly rainfall.

The most interesting note about South Korea's climate is that it's much cooler than most of the countries that also lie along the 38th parallel. While it has four seasons, the longest season is winter. The capital, Seoul, has chillier temperatures than other areas of the country, since it is based in the northern area.

This 17-minute video provides an insight into South Korea's geography. Scan the QR code with your phone to watch!

Like Japan, South Korea is famous for its springtime cherry blossoms. The Cherry Blossom Festival at Jinhae is famous.

Islands off the Korean mainland, like Jeju Island, have their own climates. These islands usually have temperatures around 10 degrees warmer than that of the mainland. That makes Jeju Island, in particular, a popular destination for a subtropical getaway. This is also where most of the country's citrus fruits come from in the winter months.

Fauna and Flora

The fauna and flora of South Korea is similar to that found in parts of China and North Korea. It's normal to see animals such as lynx, bears, and tigers. While rare, the Siberian tiger has been seen on the Korean peninsula. If you'd like to see wildcats and bears, the most likely locations include Jiri-san and Seorak-san, which are more remote and likely to provide homes for wildlife.

South Korea is also known for its own indigenous species of deer. These include the Siberian musk deer and the roe deer. The **Demilitarized** Zone, a strip of land between North and South Korea, has been left untouched since the 1950s. As a result, wildlife prospers there. The strip is a haven for animals and is particularly popular to migrating birds.

The flora in South Korea varies based on the forest zone where it can be found. For example, in the warm temperate forests, it's possible to find conifers, deciduous mixed forests, the Camellia japonica, evergreen broad-leaved trees, and pine forests. In the sub-boreal forests, visitors are more likely to see spruce trees, Korean pines, and mixed forests due to the lower temperatures. Cool temperate forests are home to some broad-leaved deciduous forests, pine trees, oak trees, and bamboo and pine forests.

Wildlife in the Demilitarized Zone

Between North and South Korea is a so-called "no man's land" that is not traversed by anyone. This border was created thanks to the armistice negotiations of the Korean War, and it has become a safe haven for animals of many species. One of these animals, the red-crowned crane, is endangered and likely only found in this thriving forest area.

The Demilitarized Zone, referred to as the DMZ, has a variety of habitats. There are mountains, marshes, wetlands, and forests. People are not allowed to go there anymore, so the animals have taken over. The Republic of Korea Ministry of Environment believes that there are around 5,097 animal and plant species that can be found in this 155-mile area. Many of them are endangered or protected by wildlife laws. It is hard to know which animals live in the DMZ since scientists aren't allowed to visit. There are landmines throughout the zone, which makes it treacherous...even if you could go there. Despite this, two rare animals, the Siberian tiger and the Amur leopard, reportedly call the area home, but there is no way to prove this. Along the DMZ is another area that has been designated as an animal sanctuary. The Peace and Life Zone is set along the buffer area that surrounds the DMZ. Visitors may go there to experience the animal life that may be found deeper in the DMZ.

The Eurasian lynx is one of several large animals native to South Korea.

RESEARCH PROJECT

Research one of South Korea's beautiful animal species. Why is it unique to this part of the world? Write a short report about the animal's place in South Korea.

TEXT-DEPENDENT QUESTIONS

1. What kinds of plants can you find in the cool, temperate forests of South Korea?

2. What is the Demilitarized Zone?

3. When is the risk of monsoons highest in South Korea?

SOUTH KOREA'S GEOGRAPHY & LANDSCAPE   17

Dol hareubangs are a series of stone statues on Jeju-do island. It is thought they date back to the eighteenth century.

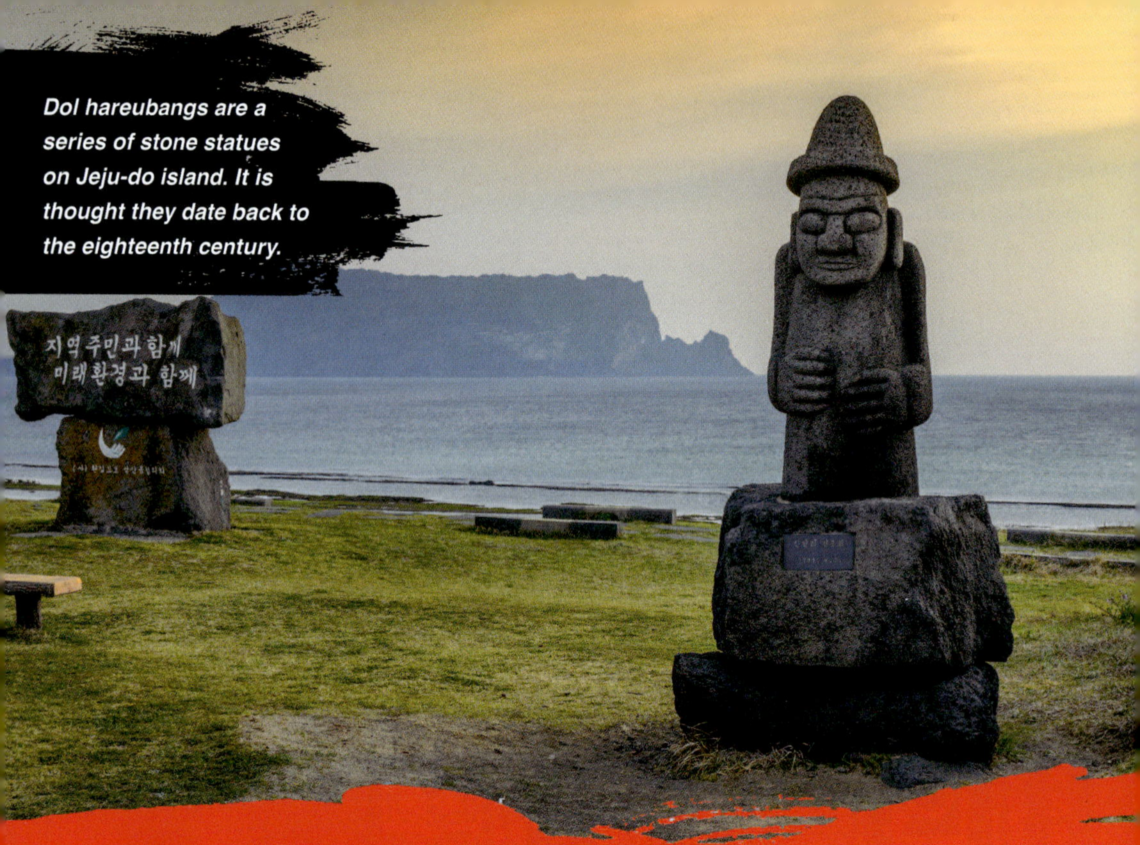

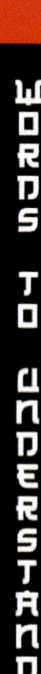

WORDS TO UNDERSTAND

democratic: supporting social equality, egalitarian

judicial: relating to the branch of government that is charged with the administration of justice

siege: a type of military operation that leads to enemy forces surrounding buildings or towns and preventing essential supplies from arriving

CHAPTER 2

THE GOVERNMENT & HISTORY OF SOUTH KOREA

South Korea, also known as the Republic of Korea, is a **democratic** republic. There are three branches of government, similar to the United States, and include the **judicial**, legislative, and executive branches. South Korea was not a country until 1948, so alone it has a short history to discuss, along with the long history during the days when it was joined with the now-separate North Korea.

A dolmen on the island of Ganghwa. Dolmens are prehistoric graves.

Early Korea: 668 CE

Korea started out as a group of competing kingdoms, but they were united into one dominion on the Korean peninsula around 668 CE. The peace was maintained over the course of thousands of years, including through the last of the ruling kingdoms. The last known ruling kingdom, the Choson Dynasty, lasted from 1392 until 1910. For the most part, the country kept to itself, though it did have to fight off invasions by Japan in the sixteenth

THE GOVERNMENT & HISTORY OF SOUTH KOREA 19

Enjoy this short video on the Annals of the Choson Dynasty, which recorded all of the dynasty's history throughout its existence.

century and Manchus in the seventeenth century. Following these invasions, there was a period of peace throughout the peninsula that lasted approximately 250 years.

Korea remained isolated until the late nineteenth century. At that point, Britain, America, and France started to work toward developing relations with Korea. Koreans were hesitant, so there were few successes for these countries.

King Taejo was the founder and the first king of the Choson Dynasty.

The Colonial Era

Beginning in the twentieth century, Russia, China, and Japan all wanted to take control of the peninsula. As a result, Korea was constantly under **siege**. Japan did eventually win control in 1905 at the tail end of the Russo-Japanese War. Korea is located in an ideal area to provide Japan with better access to Russia, which spurred the country's attempt to control the peninsula.

Korea was under colonial rule for around thirty-five years while developing into an industrial state. The Japanese tried to eliminate the indigenous culture and language during this time, which is partially why Japanese language influences are found in Korean culture today.

The old Seoul railroad station was built during Japanese rule. It is now a cultural center.

THE GOVERNMENT & HISTORY OF SOUTH KOREA

Modern History

In the 1940s, Japan was defeated by the United States. Thanks to this action, the Soviet Union and the United States split the country into two parts, best known today as North and South Korea. In August 1948, South Korea was officially established. North Korea was also established at this time, becoming the Democratic People's Republic of Korea, or the DPRK.

In 1950, South Korea declared independence from North Korea, which led to North Korea working with the Soviet Union and China to try to invade and take control of the country. South Korea was supported by the United Nations and the United States, however, which eventually resulted in an armistice agreement in 1953. It's believed that around 2 million people were killed in the Korean War.

With the armistice agreement, the Demilitarized Zone was established. It runs along the 38th parallel and is off-limits to humans.

The Choson Dynasty

The Choson Dynasty, also known as the Joseon Dynasty in some historical documents, was a Korean state founded by Taejo Yi Seong-gye. The dynasty was able to survive for around five centuries, starting at the time of the end of the Goryeo Dynasty in Kaesong. The capital was moved from Kaesong to modern-day Seoul.

The dynasty followed Confucianism, and it was the longest ruling dynasty in Korean history. Near the end of the dynasty, power struggles began to arise with international issues. Japan wanted to take over the country to secure itself and give itself a way into Russia during the Russo-Japanese War. The 1800s were also difficult for Choson due to inefficiency and corruption within the government. Along with the influence of foreigners, Korea was to be forever changed. Japan and other outside influences continued until South Korea's eventual independence in 1948.

General Park Chung-hee (wearing glasses) with U.S. President John F. Kennedy in Washington, DC on November 14, 1961.

South Korea's Fight for Democracy

The citizens of South Korea enjoyed some political freedoms in the 1950s, but in 1961, a military coup led to General Park Chung-hee gaining power. While his regime can claim success in terms of the country's rapid economic growth and industrial development, it was not to last. He was assassinated in 1979, leading to another general taking control and placing the country under martial law. That general, Chun Doo-hwan, lifted martial law in 1981 after citizens continued to fight against it. He was then elected as the country's president and a new constitution was established. He left office in 1987 when the first official election of a president took place.

The first free-vote president, Roh Tae-woo completed a series of reforms and addressed corruption in the country's government. The next year, 1988, South Korea hosted the Summer Olympic Games in Seoul.

THE GOVERNMENT & HISTORY OF SOUTH KOREA   23

Continued Democracy

Kim Young-sam, the first civilian president in over three decades, was voted into office in 1993. In 1998, Kim Dae-jung took over the presidential office and continued to work toward a peaceful democracy. In fact, he won the Nobel Peace Prize in 2000 and continues to work on economic and humanitarian aid for North Korea.

The president had a good relationship at times with the leader of North Korea, Kim Jong-il, but it deteriorated quickly when North Korea developed nuclear weapons. Relations between North and South Korea are still strained today with the volatile leader, Kim Jong-un, in charge of North Korea and its nuclear program.

In 2013, the country voted in the first female president, Park Geun-hye. Unfortunately, she was impeached in 2016, which led to the candidate Moon Jae-in taking over the role as president.

Japan in South Korea

Japan and Korea don't have a great history together. In fact, for much of the time the two countries interacted they were in a battle with one another that eventually saw Japan conquer the peninsula. Although it was common to exchange cultures and ideas throughout the centuries, Japan did eventually take control with the Japan-Korea Annexation Treaty in 1910. It was not until Japan's defeat in World War II that the combination of American and Soviet forces was able to remove Japan and agree on the dividing line that now sets North and South Korea apart.

Hirohito, Emperor of Japan in 1938.

South Korea Today

Today, South Korea is an affluent country that has been able to become nearly as affluent as China and Japan in much less time. Around half of its people live within the capital city of Seoul, with a population of approximately 25 million.

The nation continues to work toward positive relations with North Korea. In 2018, South Korea held the Winter Olympic Games during which North and South Korea marched under the same flag despite their differences. This is a good sign of the potential changes in the relationship the countries have for the better.

RESEARCH PROJECT

Write a short research paper about the changing relationship between North and South Korea.

TEXT-DEPENDENT QUESTIONS

1. What was one major cause of the strain on the relationship between North and South Korea?

2. Where do the majority of South Korean people live?

3. Which president of South Korea was awarded the Nobel Peace Prize?

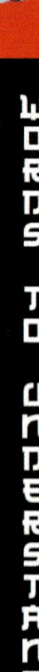

WORDS TO UNDERSTAND

domestic: within or belonging to a certain country

emerging: to become prominent or apparent

telecommunications: communication over telephone, broadcasting, cable, or telegraph

CHAPTER 3

THE SOUTH KOREAN ECONOMY

South Korea has one of the most amazing success stories of any twentieth-century country. Economically, it's one of the most successful **emerging** countries. It has great amounts of technology, and it's well developed and well connected to people around the world. Why are these achievements so impressive? Consider that in the 1960s, South Korea had one of the lowest Gross **Domestic** Products in the world and was one of the poorest countries in the world. In 2004, the country's Gross Domestic Product (GDP) surpassed $1 trillion. It's a remarkable success story, and it's one that continues to improve.

In 2018 and beyond, it's expected that South Korea will continue to grow but have slowing economic growth. It's believed that its growth will be between 2 and 3 percent yearly, which is not uncommon for advanced economies. In 2017, the official GDP was $1.54 trillion. The GDP also had a real growth rate of 3.1 percent.

Agriculture, industry and services make up the labor force. Agriculture jobs are held by 4.8 percent of the labor force, while industry consists of 24.6 percent. Services make up another 70.6 percent of the labor force.

Some of the industries in South Korea include electronics, **telecommunications**, chemicals, steel, automobile production, and shipbuilding. Only 3.7 percent of the population is unemployed.

Tourism in South Korea

Tourism is common in several of the major cities and locations including Seoul, Busan, Jeju Province, and Jeju City. Seoul draws in tourism due to its location as the capital of South Korea, while Busan is home to Haeundae Beach, other natural scenery, and temples. Hallasan Mountain, beaches, and lava tubes can be found in the Jeju Province, which is also home to Jeju City. In Jeju City, people enjoy visiting seawater saunas and the Jeju Folklore & Natural History Museum.

As the capital and a popular business location, Seoul is the cultural hub and a popular tourist destination. The N. Seoul Tower in Namsan Park is among the

Korea is a popular country to visit. These tourists are at the Gyeongbokgung palace in Seoul.

28 SOUTH KOREA

Woman selling fish at the Noryangjin Fisheries Wholesale Market in Dongjak-gu, Seoul.

The Economy of South Korea

Gross Domestic Product (GDP):
$2.035 trillion USD

Industries:
telecommunications, chemicals, automobile production, steel, shipbuilding, electronics

Agriculture:
barley, vegetables, fruit, cattle, chickens, eggs, fish, root crops, rice, milk

Export Commodities:
petrochemicals, automobile/auto parts, semiconductors, ships, wireless communication equipment, electronics, plastics, steel, computers

Export Partners:
China 25.1%, U.S. 12.2%, Vietnam 8.2%, Hong Kong 6.9%, Japan 4.7%

Import Commodities:
crude oil, semiconductors, natural gas, petroleum products, steel, computers, wireless communication equipment, fine chemicals, textiles, automobiles

Import Partners:
China 20.5%, Japan 11.5%, U.S. 10.5%, Germany 4.2%, Saudi Arabia 4.1%

Currency:
South Korean won (KRW)

Source: www.cia.gov 2017

THE SOUTH KOREAN ECONOMY   29

famous landmarks. A UNESCO World Heritage Site, Changdeokgung Palace, is also located in the city and showcases ancient architecture from the long history of the Korean people.

The majority of people who come to the country as tourists are from China, Japan and East Asia, and the Pacific, likely due to their close proximity. The total contribution of the line item "Travel & Tourism" toward the Gross Domestic Products (GDP) were 4.7 percent of total GDP in 2017 and is expected to grow in 2018.

Taxes and Other Income

South Korea has an income tax. A tax table for 2017 shows that people who earn up to 12 million KRW (South Korean Won) (US$10,560.00) pay 6 percent of their income as a tax. Another resident tax is also paid, which is 10 percent of the total income tax assessed.

South Korea's Imports and Exports

South Korea has grown into a powerhouse economically, but it still relies on some imports. It primarily brings in mineral fuels, mechanical equipment, steel, iron, and electrical equipment. The nation tends to trade with the United States, the European Union, Japan, and China.

As far as exports go, South Korea exports electronic goods, vehicles, boats and ships, machinery, and electric goods to Japan, the United States, the European Union and China.

While there has been tension between the two countries, North and South Korea do trade. Some major companies have been able to start businesses in North Korea. One of those companies is Hyundai.

Taxes in this country are based on a graduated system, so people who earn over 12 million KRW (US$10,560.00) and up to 46 million KRW (US$40,480.00) pay 15 percent plus the resident tax. Taxes grow from there to 24 percent on 46,000,001(US$40,480.01) to 88 million (US$77,440), 35 percent on 88,000,001 (US$77,440.01) to 150 million (US$132,000.00) and 38 percent on 150,000,001(US$132,000.01) to 300 million (US$264,000).

Those who earn above 300,000,001 (US$264,000.01) but less than 500 million (US$440,000) pay 40 percent plus the residency tax. This increases up to 42 percent for annual earnings of over 500 million (US$440,000). Expatriates can

As in most advanced countries, Koreans pay a level of tax according to their pay grade.

choose to have a flat 19 percent tax applied to earnings received from Korean sources.

If you are not a resident, you'll still pay the same tax rates as those residing in South Korea. People can receive personal exemptions as well as other exemptions to apply to their taxes, much like in the United States. The tax code is complex, leading many to turn to assistance when filing.

The Labor Force

The labor force in South Korea is made up of approximately 27.75 million people, based on 2017 estimates. There is a 3.7 percent estimated unemployment rate,

Samsung is a Korean multinational business employing people from all over the world.

Discover more about Korea's export-driven economy, which is made up of six primary industries.

which stayed the same year-over-year from 2016 to 2017. Around 14.4 percent of South Korea's population is below the poverty line.

Three main occupations make up the majority of employment opportunities—agricultural labor, industry labor, and services. Services are the most important to the GDP by far, accounting for 70.6 percent of the workforce. Industry makes up 24.6 percent of the workforce, while agriculture workers number 4.8 percent.

The labor force is made up of people who are fifteen years of age or older. It's important to mention that many of the younger generations have gone through full schooling, including primary and secondary education, while older generations may have had less schooling to prepare them for the labor force.

There are only a few common industries to work in. These include electronics, telecommunications, steel, shipbuilding, chemicals, and automobile production. In

THE SOUTH KOREAN ECONOMY

A tea plantation in Boseong South Jeolla Province. This area is famous for its green tea.

agriculture, products are rice, barley, vegetables, pigs, cattle, milk, eggs, fish, root crops, and chickens, to name a few. Services, such as accounting, mechanic services, restaurants, and tourism, make up the remaining job options.

Economic Sectors

The three labor force distinctions also make up the three primary economic sectors in South Korea—agricultural, services, and industrial. The nation has the eleventh largest economy in the world and the third largest in all of Asia, despite its small size. Trade and business in Korea are of the utmost importance to the GDP.

Agricultural Sector

Less than a quarter of the area in South Korea is cultivated for farming. On top of this, the percent of the country's national income dependent on agriculture has also declined. However, thanks to changes in technology and machinery, the agricultural sector has once again been growing.

One of the most important crops to the agricultural sector is rice. Fruits are also vital, as is ginseng. Commonly grown crops include tangerines, pears, strawberries, cabbages, and persimmons. Other important crops grown include barley, soybeans, potatoes, and wheat.

Agricultural development isn't just about plant life, though. Pork, milk, and beef are all important to agriculture as a result of the increased consumption of the meat and dairy products throughout the country.

Services Sector

Growth in South Korea's services sector is expected to continue to grow, since it's such a vital part of the country's GDP, focusing on tourism, entertainment, and other important services. Services currently make up 70.6 percent of all jobs for workers in the labor force, and that may continue to grow. Some services provided in the nation include retail shopping, hotels, computer services, water, electric and gas supply, media, education, and others.

The retail sector uses a large part of South Korea's workforce.

The country's services can be significantly affected by the changes in other countries, particularly in North Korea. Since tourism plays a role in South Korea's earnings, good relations between the North and South is

THE SOUTH KOREAN ECONOMY 35

considered to be vital to bringing in more tourists to the region. It's predicted that services will be the driving force behind the continued growth of the South Korean economy, since its productivity level is still just 58 percent of that found in the manufacturing sector.

Industrial Sector

The industrial sector accounts for 39.3 percent of South Korea's GDP, and it also provides around 24.6 percent of the jobs worked by the labor force. Throughout the 1980s, the progress made in the nation's economy was primarily from the industrial sector. There are a few major industries in the country, including automobile production, shipbuilding, electronics, and telecommunications.

Shipbuilding and marine engineering in Okpo in the city of Geoje in South Gyeongsang Province.

In today's economy, the automobile industry is very important. South Korea is now among the world's largest automobile manufacturers, building around 4.27 million automobiles each year. Some of the brands produced in South Korea include Hyundai, Renault, and Kia.

In telecommunications, there is also an increase in activity. Presently, there are around 40 million subscribers, making mobile telephones the largest and fastest growing area in telecommunications. There are another 20 million fixed lines among a population of around 40 million people.

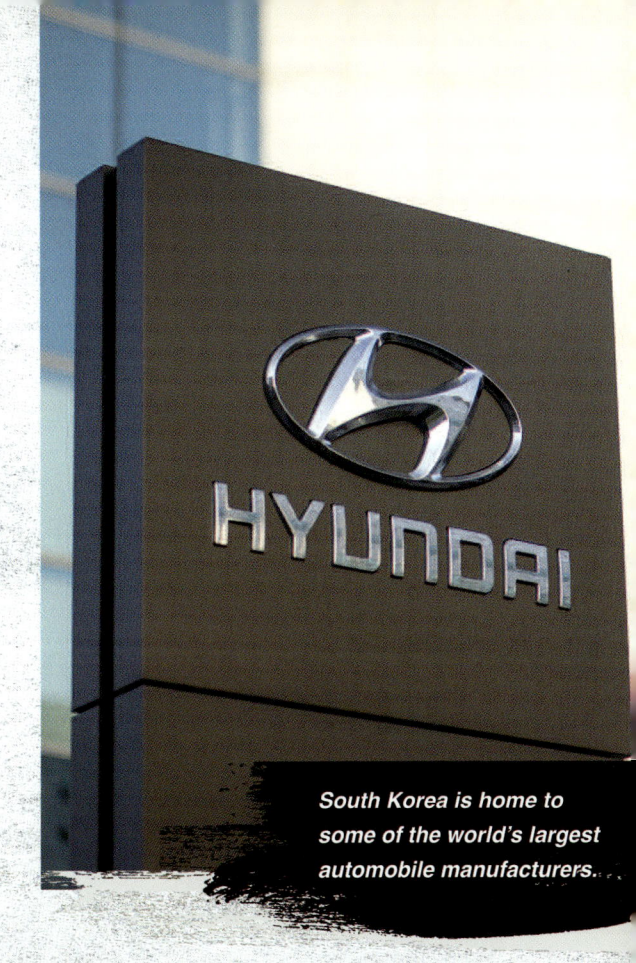

South Korea is home to some of the world's largest automobile manufacturers.

Broadband is also vital to the South Korean community and the country has the highest number of broadband users in the entire world. It strongly encourages e-commerce within the country, as well as internationally.

Ship production is another major section of the industry. South Korea has a 50.6 percent share of the shipbuilding market globally, according to recent statistics. It's home to a few of the major manufacturers, including Daewoo, STX Europe, Samsung Heavy Industries, and Hyundai Heavy Industries.

Transportation

Transportation is not much of a problem in South Korea. The country has 111 airports as of 2013 data, and 71 of those airports have paved runways. There are an additional 466 heliports, 2,472 miles of railways, and open waterways typically accessible by small watercrafts only. There are eight major ports—Busan, Gunsan, Incheon, Mokpo, Ulsan, Yeosu, Pohang, and Kwangyang.

For travelers attempting to get around the country, it's possible to take buses, subways, taxis, and trains. Each one is foreigner-friendly, with T-Money cards accepted to pay for all bus, subway, taxi, and train fares.

The South Korean Subway

The subway system in this nation is extremely convenient, and it is also cheap. There are six cities with subway systems including Daejeon, Daegu, Gwangji,

The fully automated and driverless guided transits run on the (AGT) Yongin Everline Metropolitan Subway in Seoul.

Incheon, Busan, and Seoul. The thing travelers will appreciate is that subway signs are listed in both Korean and English, making the system very friendly to foreign visitors.

Taxis

Taxis are available almost anywhere throughout the country, and they're inexpensive to use. In traffic jams, the taxi meters switch to a time basis instead of distance basis, which is something to keep in mind. Interestingly, unlike in America and some other cultures, tipping is not expected. Regular taxis are the cheapest, running around 3,300 KRW (US$2.90) for the first 1.24 miles (2 kilometers). More expensive are the deluxe taxis, which can cost up to 5,500 KRW (US$4.84) for the first 1.86 miles (3 kilometers).

Traveling by taxi is convenient, but it is more difficult for people who don't speak Korean. Many taxi drivers don't speak English, so it's a good idea to plan in advance to use a translation service, like the 1330 Tourism Help Line, to assist with translating where you'd like to go. Travelers with the ability to do so should write down the destination in Hangeul and hand it to the driver. This helps eliminate confusion.

Like in many other countries, sometimes there are surcharges and extra fares to travel in the country, and if you have to travel on highways.

Buses in South Korea

Buses are easy to use in the country, and they are found frequently throughout major cities. They're less common in rural areas, but they do still travel there in most cases. Most trips start at around 1,200 KRW (US$1.06) and increase from there, no matter how far you plan to travel. Drivers only give change in coinage, so prepare by bringing 1,000 KRW (US$0.88) notes for bus travel.

The hardest thing about the South Korean bus routes is that it's difficult to know which bus to use. Buses are not usually labeled in English, and drivers don't usually

This Seoul city bus arrives at a stop near one of the city's many Universities.

speak English. A tip is to go to a local tourist center, which is more likely to have English-speaking staff members who can help.

Taking the Train

The train system in South Korea is excellent, but as a result, it's also complex. It is not comprehensive, so it's impossible to reach every destination by train. However, most major destinations are easily reached by train travel. For those who use the train frequently, it's a good idea to get a KR pass, which allows for travel at a lower rate.

There are three train classes, Korea Train Express, Saemaeul services, and Mugunghwa trains. The first is likely to be the fastest way to the destination, while Mugunghwa trains stop the most often during travel, like a U.S. local train.

In each type of train, it's normal to find a café. There, it's possible to buy food and drinks, play games, connect to the internet, and even sing karaoke with some of the locals.

As far as costs go, the fastest Korea Train Express tickets cost around 40 percent more than Saemaeul trains. Saemaeul standard fares are twice as expensive as Mugunghwa trains. It's possible to get additional discounts through the Korail website, which is worth checking if you still have a few weeks prior to your trip. Standing tickets are also available for most journeys. Visitors and travelers can purchase Korail passes overseas before arriving in Korea.

High-speed bullet trains arrive regularly at Seoul Station.

THE SOUTH KOREAN ECONOMY 41

Economic Problems

South Korea does have a few economic problems, despite its rapid growth and development. One of the primary issues is that the economy relies heavily on international trade. As a result, inflation in neighboring countries can significantly impact the won. Another issue is that demand from China plays a major role in South Korea's ability to export. If China stops bringing in as many imports from South Korea, then around a quarter of its projected exports will be affected.

South Korea also has to contend with decisions made by the U.S. Federal Reserve. When the U.S. raises interest rates, capital begins to flow disproportionately into the United States because investors begin to ask for higher returns. The result is that there is less investment into South Korea. The only way South Korea can address this problem is by exporting more to the United States.

South Korea has a healthy economy. This is good news for its young citizens.

Yeouido is an island on the Han River in Seoul. It is Seoul's main finance and investment banking district.

RESEARCH PROJECT

Write a brief report discussing the train system in South Korea.

TEXT-DEPENDENT QUESTIONS

1. What are some problems that South Korea's economy faces today?

2. Who are South Korea's main import partners?

3. What is the most important economic sector in South Korea?

THE SOUTH KOREAN ECONOMY 43

Korean girls in traditional South Korean dress called hanbok.

WORDS TO UNDERSTAND

diaspora: a scattered population that lives in another place from their original homeland

ethnicity: a social group that shares a common and distinctive culture, religion, or language

proficiency: to have a high skill level

CITIZENS OF SOUTH KOREA—PEOPLE, CUSTOMS & CULTURE

CHAPTER 4

Ethnicities

The **ethnicities** in South Korea are fairly homogeneous. Most people are Korean, Korean-Americans, Kory-saram, those from the Korean **diaspora** who have returned, or Korean-Chinese. This is one of the most ethnically homogeneous nations in the world, with over 99 percent of the population stating that they are ethnically South Korean. Of all minorities in the country, the Chinese are the largest group and yet total only around 200,000 people.

It is possible to find other ethnicities in South Korea, though they likely did not originate there. For example, many migrants who come from Vietnam go to South Korea for marriage. North Americans tend to go to the country as tourists or business professionals. Filipinos sometimes immigrate to South Korea. In fact, it's estimated that today, around 70,000 Filipino people live in South Korea. Other foreign groups that number 5,000 or more include Thai, Sri Lankans, Taiwanese, Russians, Nepalese, and Japanese.

Language

The official language of South Korea is Korean, but it is possible to find people who speak other languages in the major cities, especially in Seoul. Standard Korean is the most prominent language. There are several dialects, including the Gyeongsang dialect, which can sound aggressive. Most people speak or understand standard Korean.

English is also spoken by many people as most Koreans under the age of forty have taken English courses at one time or another. The government aims to

English is widely spoken in South Korea, particularly by young people.

Enjoy this educational video on South Korean pop culture.

improve English **proficiency** in its people, which is why the English language has become more common.

While English is frequently known, there aren't many chances to practice it. For that reason, even if someone knows how to read, speak, or write English, they may be hesitant to speak to foreigners. In the cities this isn't always a problem, but in rural areas, it can prove difficult for travelers.

Chinese, particularly Mandarin, is a language also heard in South Korea. Since there is a large Chinese community, Cantonese may be heard as well.

In addition, Japanese is also spoken by many older residents due to the peninsula's short distance to Fukuoka. Busan's local dialect is somewhat similar to Japanese. Keep in mind, however, that older Koreans may resent the Japanese. Don't speak to an older person in Japanese unless there is no other possible language to use.

Food and Drink

Foods and drink in South Korea are often spicy, but extremely healthy and well-rounded. You can find fish dishes, vegan dishes, fermented foods, red-meat-based foods, and more. Alcohol is also common—there are over 300 traditional beverages. Some of the more common traditional alcoholic beverages include Sanseong Soju, Munbaeju, and Andong Soju. These are all forms of liquor.

The most popular traditional alcoholic beverage is rice wine, which is made with malt and steamed rice, barley, or wheat together. After fermentation, they eventually produce an alcohol of around 6 to 7 percent. Interestingly, the somewhat-mild drink is considered healthy and has been recognized for its benefits.

South Korean people believe that food is the best medicine, and it's only when your food doesn't help you feel better that you should turn to traditional medications. Korean traditions state that both illnesses and health stem from what people eat and how it's prepared. As a result, many residents will change their dietary habits to address health issues at first, only turning to traditional medicine if or when it's clear that a dietary change is not the answer.

Religion in South Korea

South Korea has followers of all the world's major religions. The most commonly found religions include Confucianism, Buddhism, and Christianity. Islam is also popular throughout the country. All of these coexist with shamanism.

Religion is not as common as in some other countries. Only around 44 percent of the Korean population subscribes to a specific religion. The most influential belief systems are Buddhism and Confucianism, both which have a long history linked throughout the country's culture. There are, for example, many Buddhist temples scattered around the country.

During the Choson Dynasty, belief in Confucianism was essential. However, it was treated more like a set of rules or morals, not as much as a religion itself. Confucianism encouraged family piety and loyalty, and the worship of ancestors.

Haedong Yonggung Buddhist temple is in Gijang-gun, Busan.

The Choson Dynasty also persecuted many Christian believers, particularly those of the Roman Catholic sect. Protestantism came to Korea in the nineteenth century, and it took hold by providing healthcare and school education to the people. Today, Protestants still operate many of the colleges, universities, medical centers, and educational institutes.

While there are Western religions throughout South Korea, there are also many native religions to learn about. Some of these include Won Buddhism, Daejonggyo, and Cheondogyo.

Education

The educational system in South Korea is impressive, to say the least. It's well known to be strong and produces results above the norm in math, science, and reading.

There was a 97.9 percent literacy rate in 2013, which has risen from a low of 22 percent in 1945, proving how far the education system has improved.

Nationally, there are approximately 19,284 teachers and around 20,261 schools, including national, public, and private institutions. There are over 11 million students, as of 2013.

Most interesting is the amount of government spending focused on education. In total, 19.8 percent of the central government's budget is allocated to the Ministry of Education, allowing for the best possible education of the population.

The government allocates a generous budget for education in South Korea.

Koreans have always had an appreciation for hard work and education. When Japan left Korea after its defeat in 1945, Koreans were left with an all-time low in literacy rates and a lack of teachers qualified to educate others. Fortunately, the Confucian cultural influences pressed Koreans to educate themselves, so they issued a series of reforms to reach a higher literacy rate.

For instance, in 1949, the Basic Education Law was enacted. By 1962, education was compulsory for children through elementary and middle school. Progress continues today, with literacy rates increasing and an educational system that is hard to match.

Looking at these facts, it's easy to see that South Koreans have access to good education. There are nine years of free compulsory education, which encourages everyone to have a basic education. For most students today, the average number of years in school will be seventeen years. The primary education enrollment percentage is around 99 percent, showing that students are getting the chance to go to school.

Kite Flying Events

While most people think of flying kites as a relaxing pastime, the reality for many Asian countries is that kite flying is an active sport. A kite can be constructed in many shapes and forms and be large, small, heavy, ornate, flat, or of another structure. They're flown in sporting events, especially throughout Asian communities. You may also know this sport as "kite fighting," which is an apt name.

In a kite flying match, two kite flyers compete with one another. The goal is to cut the other person's line, not to damage the kite itself. In some cases, many people compete at the same time to see who will become the victor. In some variations, the goal is to snag the opponent's kite and drag it down so it will fall.

Interestingly, players in Asian countries coat their lines with abrasive materials so they're better able to cut opponent's lines. Some lines have metal knives or finely crushed glass applied to them, which are used to snip through the opponents' lines. The kite tails may also have sharp objects attached to them.

This is a somewhat dangerous sport, as you may imagine. Some countries now ban or restrict the use of abrasive materials on the kite lines and have outlawed certain materials that were previously used in kite fighting.

South Korean soccer fans at the FIFA World Cup competition in Russia in 2018.

When looking at the sixteen years of average education for women and eighteen years for men, it's possible to assume that women generally finish all twelve years of primary and secondary school before four years of college or similar education. Men take an additional two years due to having a two-year military service requirement in the Republic of Korea (ROK) Armed Forces—army, navy, or air force.

After high school, education is no longer free, so some people's ability to continue their education is limited and fewer people go onto university as a result. However, there is another issue at play, which is that local jobs are hiring those who haven't gone on to college. Those without advanced education find it fairly easy to be hired. With these prospects, some students go directly into the workforce instead of to college.

Sports

South Korea has an affinity for sports, with its major contribution being tae kwon do. The nation doesn't only appreciate martial arts, though, and the sports the population enjoys are becoming Westernized over time. Kite flying, wrestling, and bull fighting are popular. In Asia, many different countries participate in kite flying as a sport.

South Koreans also enjoy participating in baseball and soccer (called football in Asia). Their national football team was able to reach the FIFA World Cup semi-finals in 2002, making them the first Asian Football Confederation member to do so. Since 1986, the country has qualified for every World Cup played, showing just how amazing its teams are. And as baseball has become popular, South Korean players attend the World Baseball Classic and are among the best in the league.

Kite flying is a popular pastime in South Korea.

South Korea has also hosted several major sporting events including the 2002 FIFA World Cup and the 1988 Summer Olympics. It also hosted the 2015 Presidents Cup in Incheon, the 2014 Asian Games in Incheon, and the 2015 Summer World Military Games.

Traditional sports in South Korea include jokgu, ssireum, and tae kwon do. Jokgu is a sport similar to a mixture of football and volleyball. Ssireum is a type of wrestling that has the aim of toppling the upper body of the opponent to the ground.

Tae kwon do is a Korean martial art that is extremely popular all over South Korea.

The Arts: Architecture, Painting, Music, and Literature

It is safe to say that the South Korean people appreciate the arts and culture. In fact, recent years have brought about governmental changes that hope to encourage more people to remember their heritage. Although the population has gone through major changes, they are encouraged to look into the past.

Perhaps the most fortunate thing about South Korea is that there are large collections of literary pieces, musical records, paintings, and recordkeeping that make it easier to look into the past. Here's a little more about what to expect in South Korean architecture, painting, music, and literature.

Architecture

If you go to South Korea, you'll notice rows of industrial buildings. These buildings, known as *danji*, are a result of the utilitarian designs created after World War II. After that conflict, the United States invested in the country and helped it rebuild. Unfortunately, the helpful money that was used to industrialize and modernize the country didn't incorporate South Korean design elements into buildings. Instead, the focus was on essential repairs that occurred alongside quick, cheap, and simple

The temples at Bulguksa are examples of traditional Korean architecture. The site dates back to 528 CE.

Bukchon Hanok Village in Seoul is an example of traditional village architecture.

designs for homes. Many of the traditional Hanok villages were razed. In their place are now uniform buildings with simple construction, and the majority were not designed with longevity in mind.

The good news is that South Korea has been investing in better design in the last decade and plans to continue in the future. With one of the strongest economies in the world, the nation has the financial backing to invest. Many local architects went abroad to study and have returned with sophisticated skills in design and construction, so new buildings are often progressive and some have unusual shapes or styles. Contemporary style seems to be the new South Korean style. One example of this is the Floating Islands, which is located in Seoul. These three manmade islands include a moonlight trail and performance hall, cultural experience center, and water leisure activities. At night, each of these unique structures is illuminated and has live light shows, drawing in tourism.

Another example of distinctive architecture is the Busan Cinema Center, designed by Coop Himmelblau. The structure has an unusual roof design that is unsupported across a large patio space. Individuals who come to the theater can watch a movie on the roof, making for a unique experience.

The Dongdaemun Design Plaza is a major development landmark in Seoul. It was designed by Zaha Hadid.

Dating back to the Choson Dynasty, this painting is called the Lovers Under the Moon.

Painting

Korean paintings date as far back as the art on the walls of Goguryeo tombs. The visual art from the peninsula is traditionally spontaneous, natural, and simple. Korean art was highly influenced by the Chinese and their artistic endeavors, so there are some similarities between the two.

The Golden Age of Painting occurred during the Choson period, when Confucianism was also the primary religious context that people adhered to throughout their daily lives. Minwha paintings were produced by amateurs and folk artists around the country as painting became a common daily activity. Korean painters often chose to paint scenery and portraits of people doing everyday tasks.

Unfortunately, much of the artwork that was produced in South Korea following this period was suppressed as a result of Japan's occupation, which led to the country rapidly modernizing. This also means that the current art style is one that is more recognizable as an international style, not a traditionally Korean style.

The first Korean painting was dated at around 108 CE, but between then and the Choson period, there were many different styles that were affected by Chinese influences and the impact of other topics, like Buddhism and celestial observations. One of the most important facts is that the majority of notable Japanese painters

A traditional painting on the wall of a temple in Changnyeong.

Traditional music being played at a Confucian ceremony called Seokjeon Daeje in Jeonju Hanok Village.

were known to be from South Korea or trained by Koreans in their arts. These happened during the Baekje era, a period of time when art was at its most influential.

Music

Traditionally, Korean music was influenced by the Mongols and Chinese. The earliest type of music was shaman music, which could be heard in the third century CE. Singing and dancing among the northwestern Korean tribes was a common part of life and often performed during agricultural festivals.

Shamanistic music uses a variety of instruments, including gongs, wooden drums with single heads, and the changgo, an hourglass-shaped drum with two heads. It's struck by a stick or beater on the right, but the player uses their hand on the left side.

During shaman rituals, it was also normal to see flutes, fiddles, and double-reed wind instruments.

One of the earliest instruments mentioned is the globular flute, which is among the oldest artifacts of Chinese music. The double-reed aerophone is also an instrument unique to Korea, both North and South.

Today, South Korea is probably best known in the international sphere for its unique pop music, better known as "K-pop." Pop music began to take hold in the 1940s and 50s, with the oldest form known as *teuroteu*—a kind of foxtrot music.

Hip-hop artist Yoon Mi-rae and her husband, rapper Tiger JK, are credited with popularizing American-style hip-hop in South Korea.

Today, K-pop has taken on a few styles but is inspired by R&B and hip-hop. Its popularity is also called the "Korean Wave," which is boosted by TV dramas using band members and their songs as actors and soundtracks for the series.

Don't forget more traditional music, though, like the opera. Korea has embraced Western-style opera. In fact, many famous singers in the opera are from Korea. Korean opera singers have become world-renowned in some cases.

South Korea established the National Opera Group in 1968, and since then, the country has been openly grooming performers to sing in operas within and outside the country. Opera and music are so important to some that they will travel abroad to study opera during school. Some common places to travel include France, Germany, and Italy, where many of the famous opera houses still stand today.

Literature

Korean literature began long ago, influenced by classical Chinese and eventually developing into Hangul, the national alphabet of Korea. Korea had its own language for several thousand years, but despite that, writers often used the Chinese language alphabet for writing until the development of its own alphabet in the mid-fifteenth century.

After the development of the Unified Silla Dynasty in 668, Koreans were educated in reading the Confucian Classics as well as Chinese literature and history. This created a unique phenomenon where the upper class could speak Korean but were also able to speak Chinese that they learned through writing.

There are some unique poetry styles that come from Korea. One is the hyangga, which is a poem written with four, eight, or ten lines. The poems were typically constructed by Buddhists or students of Hwarangdo.

Pyolgok is another form of poetry that is characterized by having a refrain in the middle or at the end of the stanza. Sijo, a third form, is the most popular and enduring form of poetry. These are three-line poems with fourteen or sixteen syllables in each line. These poems were made famous during the Choson period.

Finally, there is a fourth style, the kasa. This is a longer arrangement that is usually written in couplets.

In prose, it was common to see fiction pieces, myths, legends, and folktales. Thanks to the historical records kept, many of the great historical narratives are found in these historical records, preserved to this day.

Oral prose was also common, using puppetry or ballads to transmit information and stories. Masked plays were conducted with five actors.

RESEARCH PROJECT

Create a short presentation about the arts in South Korea. Next, choose a special South Korean building, painting, or other work of art and document its history.

TEXT-DEPENDENT QUESTIONS

1. Why do most young people in South Korea speak English?

2. Why is Mandarin spoken by some people in South Korea?

3. Name the most common religions in South Korea.

The capital city of South Korea is Seoul.

WORDS TO UNDERSTAND

authentic: genuine and undisputed

boutiques: small, sophisticated or fashionable stores

jjimjilbang: a type of sauna and spa

karaoke: a form of entertainment in which a device plays music to which a person sings along

SOUTH KOREA

CHAPTER 5

FAMOUS CITIES OF SOUTH KOREA

Seoul

Seoul is the capital of South Korea, located in the north of the country. It traditionally had an industrial feel, but it has been able to change that image into a location filled with parks, design, and culture. Beautiful landscaping is common throughout the city, as are **boutiques** and cafes that are popular among travelers and locals.

Seoul is home to approximately 10 million people. It is also home to several World Heritage sites, including the Seoul City Wall, and the alleys between Hanok and the Jongmyo shrine.

What makes Seoul so popular among travelers is that it is a 24-hour city. That means that there is something open at all times, day or night—night markets, street tent vendors, and self-service **karaoke** bars. Many people stop at the **jjimjilbang** for rest—a sauna and spa. It's easy to stay out all night in Seoul with so many things to do.

From Seoul, it's possible to reach the Demilitarized Zone, and it's also easy to reach Incheon, to the west. Suwon, to the south, also has several World Heritage sites.

Perhaps the most important thing about Seoul is that it has amazing public transportation, much of which is foreigner-friendly. It's easy to travel beyond the city's limits, so there's no excuse not to.

Incheon

Incheon is an interesting and old city that has existed since approximately 475 CE. It was only named Incheon in 1413, being known before that as Soseonghyeon, and by other names even before this time.

Jongmyo in Seoul is the oldest and most authentic of the Confucian royal shrines to have been preserved.

Enjoy this short video featuring several of the famous locations in Incheon.

    Incheon has everything tourists need to explore the beautiful culture of South Korea. It hosted the 2014 Asian Games and has gone through a real-estate development phase that has updated the face of the city. Visitors may enjoy heading to the Bupheong District, where they can visit designer shops. Others might like the local history of Liberty Park or to go down to Chinatown for **authentic** cuisine. Incheon is linked to nearby islands by way of ferry, which makes it easy for visitors to go out on daytrips if they want to get away from the hustle and bustle of the city.

    It's easy to get to Incheon, especially since it is home to an international airport. The city itself is located in the northwest, and its name stands for "kind river." It sits on the coast, allowing an active international port to flourish. As a coastal city, it is ideally placed to continue to grow. Presently it is added together with the Gyeonggi Province and Seoul to form the fifth largest megapolis in the world (by population).

FAMOUS CITIES OF SOUTH KOREA

Incheon's Chinatown is South Korea's only official Chinatown. It is in Jung-gu and dates to 1884.

Suwon

Many people outside Asia are not familiar with Suwon, but it is a location that should be known. As the largest city in the Gyeonggi-do province, it is home to several World Heritage sites. At one point, Suwon was considered as a potential capital of then-unified Korea, but the ruler of the Choson Dynasty at that time passed away before transferring power to the region.

Located approximately nineteen miles south of Seoul, it's a quick trip from one city to the next. For people planning to visit Suwon for a few days, the hotels in Hwaseong are known as great places to stop. They're in a good location and offer positive experiences. When you're ready to get something to eat, try galbi, the region's specialty. Galbi is translated roughly into "beef ribs," and Suwon is renowned for its version. It's common to find the native food in restaurants, especially in Yeonpo Galbi.

Adults who are interested in nightlife may find that Suwon has less to offer than Seoul, but it does still have 24-hour offerings—bars, local pubs known as *hof*, and karaoke rooms that can be rented for the night. Most of these are located to the east of the rail station. For a day in Suwon, estimated costs for the hotel, street food, and

Hwaseong is a fortress dating from the Choson Dynasty. It surrounds the center of Suwon.

subway can be as low as 100,000 won, which equals around US$89 as of January 2019. For a high-end experience, travelers should set aside up to 300,000 won, or US$267.

Daegu

Located in Gyeongsabgbuk-do, Daegu is the fourth largest city in South Korea. It's progressive and interesting for travelers since it is one of the few places with traditional medicine markets. For people interested in Korea's heritage, this is the city to see.

This is also a popular destination for exchange students and English teachers, so it's normal to run into other English-speaking people there. This is a student-heavy city, which means that the entire city has a youthful buzz as a result.

It's easy to get around Daegu. There is a subway with three lines, each of which can help you travel to local areas like Haein-sa or Jikji-sa, which are good locations for

Mr. Sunshine in Daegu

A popular Korean series came to America in 2018. Titled "Mr. Sunshine," the series was about life during the late Choson era (referred to as "Joseon" in the series). What's most interesting about the drama is that the locations where it was filmed have all been preserved for tourism. It's possible to visit the set, as well as several historical locations used in the series. Some of those historical locations include the Choganjeong Garden, which has a famous pavilion built in 1582. Another area used in the series was part of Keimyung University's Hanhakchon Village, a picturesque setting for a historical drama as well as for tourists, students, and others. This is just one additional place to stop by while in South Korea, especially for those who are fans of the series' Netflix release.

daytrips to temples. The area is picturesque, and it is often used for the setting of dramas, especially historical fiction.

Since this is more of a youthful city, it's no surprise that there is a busy downtown district with lots to do at night. There are literally hundreds of nightclubs, cafes, and bars to choose from, and those who love craft beer experiences may travel here for the offerings of the district.

Busan

Busan was previously known as Pusan and is a major metropolitan city in South Korea. It's the second most populated city, after Seoul, as it is home to approximately 3.5 million people.

A night view of the E-World theme park and the 83 Tower in Daegu.

Traditional wooden houses at the Daegu Otgol Village. It is a popular tourist attraction.

    Busan is an important city due to its role as a cultural, educational, and economic center of the southeast. Its port is only around 120 miles from two Japanese islands, Honshu and Kyushu, providing the city with a great location for international trade. Its port, the Port of Busan, was established in 1876 and is now South Korea's busiest port, and also the ninth busiest harbor in the world.

    Busan was one of only two cities that were not occupied by North Korea during the Korean War, between 1950 and 1953. As a result, the Port of Busan became a self-governing city immediately after the Korean War. Today, it is home to many industries, including automobile manufacturing, shipbuilding, and electronic, steel, chemical, and paper industries (among others).

Near the Port of Busan is a second harbor that was designed to relieve congestion. Known as Busan New Port, it was finished in December 2011.

People visiting Busan don't necessarily want to spend all their time in the port city, so it's a good idea to get to know some adventurous things to do in the area.

The impressive skyline of Busan and the Gwangandaegyo Bridge.

Popular for visitors are sites such as Taejongdae, which is an elevated park and lighthouse; Haedong Yonggungsa, a seaside Buddhist temple from the fourteenth century; and Haeundae Beach, a fun area for individuals and families who wish to spend time near the water.

Tourists often enjoy Busan because of the many Buddhist temples located in the mountains. One of them, Beomeosa Temple, is one of the most popular in the area.

Yeongdo Lighthouse is situated in Taejongdae park.

Beomeosa Temple in Busan.

RESEARCH PROJECT

Create a short visual guide to the five major cities in South Korea.

TEXT-DEPENDENT QUESTIONS

1. What are three landmarks to visit in the famous cities of South Korea?

2. What are a few ethnic groups found in South Korea?

3. Where would you be able to find Taejongdae, and what could you do there?

The Port of Busan is South Korea's largest seaport where most of its goods leave and arrive.

WORDS TO UNDERSTAND

mass media: the media viewed by the masses (the population), including radio, television, and other forms of broadcasting

portfolio: a portable case for holding material; items collected together in a group; financially, a range of investments held by a country, business, or individual

renewable: not depleted when used; automatically replenished

A BRIGHT FUTURE FOR SOUTH KOREA

CHAPTER 6

China's Influence

China has had many centuries of influence on South Korea, sharing painting, ceramics, and other cultural elements with the country. Today, China is most closely linked to South Korea through the economy. These two nations trade with one another, and the amount of imports and exports can directly affect South Korea's won. For example, if China stops importing from South Korea, it could significantly impact the country's GDP. However, some believe that China also negatively impacts South Korea because of its ability to manufacture similar goods and undermine South Korea's growth. Others believe China is a growing nation with much importance, going as far as to send their children there to study and learn from the country's best schools.

There are some worries that South Korea might be too dependent on trade with China since it depends on China for around half of its growth annually. Out of all the goods it sent around the world, US$125 billions' worth were sent to China, while the remaining US$375 billion were sent to other countries. Clearly, the two countries have close ties when it comes to trade.

While South Korea is among the largest economies in the world, that doesn't mean that it can't be influenced by others. In reality, it may be influenced more because of its rapid growth and dependency on trade with foreign nations. If any trades fail, or if the profits are reduced, then the GDP takes an immediate hit.

South Korea's Economy

As one of the best in the world, its freedom index is 73.8 percent, which means it's the 27th freest in the world as of 2018. When ranked among forty-three countries in the Asia-Pacific region, South Korea is listed as the seventh.

Currently, the majority of South Korea's energy comes from coal, although the government is taking action to replace this with renewable energies.

The nation is currently investing in income-led growth, which means that it aims to reduce debt within households, boost taxes on the wealthy and corporations, and increase the minimum wage to continue to help its population rise out of poverty.

Trade is significant to South Korea's economy. In fact, 78 percent of its GDP is based on imports and exports combined. Tariff rates are set at around 4.8 percent, bringing in income for the country. Of all the sectors in business, banking is one of the most stable, which is a positive sign for the continued growth of the economy.

Renewable Energy in South Korea

South Korea currently obtains around 21 percent of its electricity from nuclear fuel. Another 2 percent comes from hydroelectric plants, and another 8 percent of electricity is collected from **renewable** resources not named. Presently, coal and nuclear power make up around 70 percent of the country's electrical supply.

Renewables make up approximately 6 percent directly, with wind and solar contributing only around 1 percent of the supply.

South Korea intends to increase its renewable resources, though. The country aims to fulfill 20 percent of its energy needs with renewable energy by 2030. To do that, the country will continue to install renewable power generators such as solar panels and wind turbines. It plans to add 30.8 gigawatts of solar energy and another 16.5 gigawatts of wind energy to its **portfolio**, hoping to meet the growing needs of the nation's population in the coming years.

Culture Spending

South Korea does appreciate the arts and culture. Recently, the government increased the culture budget by over 10 percent. The Ministry of Culture, Sports and Tourism is in charge of cultural experiences, education, and more within the country's borders. The central government also spends funds on many other different aspects of culture. The goal in South Korea is to continue to bring culture to the everyday lives of its citizens. The money also goes toward promoting tourism and sports, generating jobs, and helping increase Korean **mass media** worldwide.

South Korea Today and into the Future

Today, this unique, powerful nation continues to surprise the world. It has a strong economy and has been making waves globally with its K-dramas and K-pop groups. It's expanding its reach through music, art, and culture, as well as through trade. Many people believe that South Korea is still finding its place on the world stage, but it is making good headway. It's one of few countries able to grow at such an astounding rate. It's referred to as a "miracle" when compared to other Asian countries that are also attempting to grow into stronger countries.

Geographically, South Korea is located between China, Japan, and Russia, which puts it in a difficult situation when faced with challenges, but also gives it an ideal location for trade and economic benefits.

South Korea's economy is continuing to grow which is good news for its citizens.

When it comes to technology and manufacturing, South Korea has become mighty. It is willing to invest in research, spending more of its GDP on research than other major countries, such as the United States or Germany. This research helps it reduce costs, improve profit margins, and continue its astounding growth.

While South Korea struggles with matching China's low costs or Japan's high quality items, it has been able to match up value for quality, making it a strong contender in trade circles. It also continues to expand tax deductions for businesses who invest in research and development, encouraging continued exploration of opportunities that may appear.

It's true that the nation can't rely on manufacturing to maintain its economy forever, so it is investing in the services sector, which has the most potential for job growth. People will need good jobs as technology continues to advance throughout the country.

It's believed that South Korea can continue to grow at a rate of around 4 percent yearly, which is something to continue to look forward to.

RESEARCH PROJECT

Discuss the importance of increasing jobs in the services sector as technology continues to improve. How does technology affect job availability?

TEXT-DEPENDENT QUESTIONS

1. In what year does South Korea plan to boost its renewable energy over 20 percent?

2. How does China impact South Korea?

3. How does South Korea's government plan to continue helping households in the country?

SOUTH KOREAN FOOD

Food on the peninsula is sometimes spicy and typically healthy. Long ago, people believed that what you ate made a difference in your health, so food and medicine have the same function in the Korean lifestyle. Fermentation is extremely common because it preserves more of the nutrients in food and makes sure the human body can absorb them more fully.

Hot and spicy foods are common in South Korea, especially using chilies. Fresh seafood is often used in combination with rice dishes and spicy meats.

Two of the most famous South Korean dishes are bibimbop and kimchi. Bibimbap is simply a mixed rice dish, while kimchi is a form of fermented, spiced cabbage. Both can be prepared at home by following these recipes.

South Korean Bibimbap

Makes 4 servings

Ingredients

Meat and meat sauce
4 ounces beef mince
1 tablespoon soy sauce
1 teaspoon sugar
¼ teaspoon minced garlic
1 tablespoon sesame oil

Vegetables and mix-ins
4 ounces zucchini
4 ounces carrots
½ teaspoon sea salt
3 to 4 servings of steamed rice (sticky)
3 to 4 eggs
Cooking oil
4 ounces bean sprouts
4 ounces seasoned spinach

Bibimbap sauce
2 tablespoons gochujang
1 tablespoon water
1 tablespoon sugar
1 tablespoon roasted sesame seeds
1 teaspoon vinegar
1 tablespoon sesame oil
1 teaspoon minced garlic

Directions

1. Mix the beef together with the meat sauce ingredients above. Allow the meat to marinate and then cook on a medium heat until cooked through.

2. Leave the meat aside and then mix the bibimbap sauce ingredients together in a bowl. Put it aside.

3. Rinse, peel, and julienne the carrots. Add a pinch of sea salt to the carrots and cook for 2 to 3 minutes on medium high heat until soft.

4. Next, boil the spinach. Once soft, place it aside in a bowl and add a small amount of sesame oil and sesame seeds.

5. Bring the beansprouts to a boil, drain and add a pinch of sea salt and sesame oil or seeds to taste.

6. Following this, julienne the zucchini and add them to the wok. Add cooking oil and a pinch of sea salt. Cook them until the are al dente (still firm).

7. Place steamed rice into a bowl and add meat, the assorted vegetables, and bibimbap sauce.

8. Serve with a fried egg with a runny yoke on top.

SOUTH KOREAN FOOD 83

Easy-to-Make Kimchi

Makes 8

Ingredients

10 pounds napa cabbage
½ cup sweet rice flour
¼ cup sugar
3 cups water
1–2 tablespoons ginger
1 cup minced onion
1 cup crushed garlic
1 cup fish sauce
1 cup hot pepper flakes
2 cups leek
10 green onions
2 cups Korean radish
¼ cup carrot
1 cup salt
⅔ lb. fresh squid

Directions

1. Start by cutting out any discolored cabbage leaves. Then cut the cabbage lengthwise into four quarters. The cores should be removed.

2. Next, soak the cabbage in a large basin using cold water. Sprinkle it with salt. For 10 pounds of cabbage, one cup of salt is sufficient.

3. Every 30 minutes for the next 1½ hours, turn the cabbage. After 90 minutes, rinse the cabbage in cold water at least three times to remove all the salt. Set the cabbage aside after draining.

4. Directions to make kimchi porridge: Use 3 cups water and ½ cup sweet rice flour to create a mixture in a pot. Bring them to a boil and stir until bubbles appear (approximately 5 minutes). Add ¼ cup sugar to the mixture and stir it for several more minutes until it appears translucent. Allow this to cool.

5. Directions to make kimchi paste: Take the fully cooled porridge and place it into a large bowl. Add all the ingredients one at a time: 1 cup fish sauce, 1 cup crushed garlic, ¼ cups of hot pepper flakes, 1 cup of minced onion, and up to 2 tablespoons of minced ginger. Blend the ingredients together.

6. Now it's time to add the squid, but first wash, drain, and chop the squid to prepare it for the paste. Add it to the paste once prepared and chopped. Add 10 green onions sliced diagonally, 2 cups of chopped leeks, and a quarter cup of julienned carrot. Add 2 cups of julienned Korean radish.

7. Mix these ingredients together until the kimchi paste is done. Finally, mix the cabbage with the kimchi paste by the handfuls, doing so carefully.

8. Then place the kimchi into an air-tight, sealed plastic bag, container, or jar. It's possible to eat the kimchi fresh or after it has fermented, depending on your preference.

9. Place the kimchi containers in the refrigerator, where they'll ferment more slowly but retain a fresher taste.

10. Traditional methods include fermenting the kimchi for a longer period of time in a cool spot, such as clay pots placed in the ground.

FESTIVALS & HOLIDAYS

There are a variety of holidays in South Korea. These include:

New Year's Day (Jan. 1)

Seollal (Feb. 4th through the 6th)

Independence Movement Day (Mar. 1)

Children's Day (May 5)

Buddha's Birthday (May 12)

Memorial Day (June 6)

Liberation Day (Aug. 15)

Chuseok (Sept. 12th through the 14th)

National Foundation Day (Oct. 3)

Hangeul Day (Oct. 9)

Christmas (Dec. 25)

Each of these holidays is an official Korean holiday, meaning that banks and offices are closed. Most of the time, palaces, restaurants, shopping malls, amusement facilities, and museums remain open on holidays so families and friends have places to go together. Interestingly, most people in Korea travel to their hometowns during the holidays instead of staying wherever they currently reside.

Of these holidays, there are a few not common in other countries. Seollal is one, which is Lunar New Year's Day and celebrates family ties. Families dress up in their best clothing and reaffirm their family relations. They spend time together and fly kites, spin tops, or play other games.

Another uncommon holiday in Western countries is Children's Day, on which children and their parents celebrate the hope of growing up strong and healthy. Parents take their children to movies, parks, or amusement parks on this day, as an example, to spend time together. Buddha's Birthday is widely celebrated throughout Asia. This is always on the eighth day of the fourth lunar month, so the date changes from year to year. The most obvious sign of the celebration are rows of lanterns leading to the Buddhist temples.

Liberation Day is a very important holiday, celebrating the independence of South Korea and Japan's acceptance of the terms of surrender in 1945.

National Foundation Day, which many confuse with Liberation Day, is actually the date when Koreans believe their nation was founded by the god-king Dangun. Ceremonies are held throughout the country, with the main celebration at the top of Manisan Mountain on Ganghwado Island.

Finally, the last holiday likely unknown by Western cultures is Hangeul Day. This is the day that celebrates the creation of the country's native alphabet in the publication of Hunminjeongeum in 1446.

The Seoul Lantern Festival is an annual festival held every November in Seoul. Hundreds of lanterns decorate the public recreation space of Cheonggyecheon.

FESTIVALS & HOLIDAYS 87

Series Glossary of Key Terms

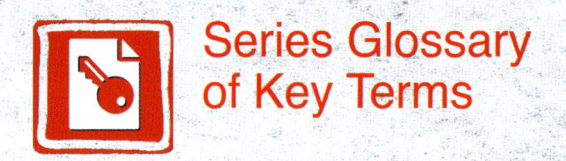

aboriginal	Of or relating to the original people living in a region.
archaeology	A science that deals with past human life and activities as shown by objects (as pottery, tools, and statues) left by ancient peoples.
archipelago	A group of islands.
biomass	A renewable energy source from living or recently living plant and animal materials, which can be used as fuel.
Borneo	An island of the Malay Archipelago southwest of the Philippines and divided between Brunei, Malaysia, and Indonesia.
boundary	Something that indicates or fixes a limit or extent.
Buddhism	A religion of eastern and central Asia based on the teachings of Gautama Buddha.
Christianity	A religion based on the teachings of Jesus Christ.
civilization	An advanced stage (as in art, science, and government) in the development of society.
colony	A distant territory belonging to or under the control of a nation.
commodity	Something produced by agriculture, mining, or manufacture.
Confucianism	Of or relating to the Chinese philosopher Confucius or his teachings or followers.
culture	The habits, beliefs, and traditions of a particular people, place, or time.
dialect	A form of a language that is spoken in a certain region or by a certain group.
diversity	The condition or fact of being different.
economic boom	A period of increased commercial activity within either a business, market, industry, or economy as a whole.
emerging market	An emerging market economy is a nation's economy that is progressing toward becoming advanced.
endangered species	A species threatened with extinction.
enterprise	A business organization or activity.
European Union	An economic, scientific, and political organization consisting of 27 European countries.
foreign exchange reserve	Foreign currency reserves that are held by the central bank of a country.
geothermal energy	Energy stored in the form of heat beneath the earth's surface. It is a carbon-free, renewable, and sustainable form of energy.
global warming	A warming of the earth's atmosphere and oceans that is thought to be a result of air pollution.

Hindu	A person who follows Hinduism.
independence	The quality or state of not being under the control of, reliant on, or connected with someone or something else.
industrialization	The widespread development of industries in a region, country, or culture.
infrastructure	The system of public works of a country, state, or region.
interest rate	The proportion of a loan that is charged as interest to the borrower, typically expressed as an annual percentage of the loan outstanding.
Islam	The religious faith of Muslims including belief in Allah as the sole deity and in Muhammad as his prophet.
land reclamation	The process of creating new land from oceans, riverbeds, or lake beds.
landmass	A large area of land.
Malay	A member of a people of the Malay Peninsula, eastern Sumatra, parts of Borneo, and some adjacent islands.
Mandarin	The chief dialect of China.
maritime	Of or relating to ocean navigation or trade.
Mongol	A member of any of a group of traditionally pastoral peoples of Mongolia.
monsoon	The rainy season that occurs in southern Asia in the summer.
mortality rate	The number of a particular group who die each year.
natural resource	Something (as water, a mineral, forest, or kind of animal) that is found in nature and is valuable to humans.
peninsula	A piece of land extending out into a body of water.
precipitation	Water that falls to the earth as hail, mist, rain, sleet, or snow.
recession	A period of reduced business activity.
republic	A country with elected representatives and an elected chief of state who is not a monarch and who is usually a president.
Ring of Fire	Belt of volcanoes and frequent seismic activity nearly encircling the Pacific Ocean.
Shintoism	The indigenous religion of Japan.
street food	Prepared or cooked food sold by vendors in a street or other public location for immediate consumption.
sultan	A ruler especially of a Muslim state.
Taoism	A religion developed from Taoist philosophy and folk and Buddhist religion and concerned with obtaining long life and good fortune often by magical means.
tiger economy	A tiger economy is a nickname given to several booming economies in Southeast Asia.
typhoon	A hurricane occurring especially in the region of the Philippines or the China Sea.
urbanization	The process by which towns and cities are formed and become larger as more and more people begin living and working in central areas.

Chronology

1945: The Japanese occupation of Korea ends, spurring changes in the region.
1948: The Republic of Korea is proclaimed.
1950: South Korea declares its independence, which causes the North Korean invasion and the Korean War.
1960: President Syngman Ree steps down after accusations of electoral fraud. The Second Republic is formed as a result.
1961: General Park Chung-hee takes over in a military coup.
1963: The Third Republic is created and industrial development increases.
1972: Martial law begins.
1991: South Korea joins the United Nations.
1993: Kim Young-sam is elected as the first civilian president.
1998: Kim Dae-jung becomes president and enacts the Sunshine Policy to provide aid to North Korea.
2000: Kim Dae-jung awarded the Nobel Peace Prize.
2000: Summit in Pyongyang between South and North Korea. Border liaison offices open in Panmunjom, a truce village. Prisoners numbering 3,500 are granted amnesty by South Korea.
2002: Roh Moo-hyun wins presidential election.
2007: North and South Korea agree to restart peace talks.
2007: North and South Korea come to an agreement on a free-trade deal.
2007: Lee Myung-bak wins presidential election.
2009: Warships from the North and South exchange fire at a sea border under dispute.
2012: South Korea elects its first female president, Park Geun-hye.
2013: South Korea launches a satellite into orbit.
2017: Moon Jae-in is elected president in landslide election.
2018: Kim Jong-un enters South Korea, becoming the first to do so. He meets with President Moon Jae-in to discuss the end of hostile actions.

Further Reading

Hong, Euny. *The Birth of Korean Cool: How One Nation Is Conquering the World Through Pop Culture.* Picador, 2014.

Lafayette De Mente, Boye. *Etiquette Guide to Korea: Know the Rules that Make the Difference!* Tuttle Publishing, 2017.

Richmond, Simon, et al. *Lonely Planet Korea (Travel Guide).* Lonely Planet, 2016.

Snyder, Scott A. *South Korea at the Crossroads: Autonomy and Alliance in an Era of Rival Powers (A Council on Foreign Relations Book).* Columbia University Press, 2018.

Internet Resources

https://www.lonelyplanet.com/south-korea
South Korea Travel Information and Travel Guide.

http://english.visitkorea.or.kr/enu/index.kto
Imagine Your Korea.

https://vkc.or.kr/
Visit Korea Committee.

https://www.cia.gov/library/publications/the-world-factbook/geos/ks.html
CIA World Factbook.

The websites listed on this page were active at the time of publication. The publisher is not responsible for websites that have changed their addresses or discontinued operation since the date of publication. The publisher will review and update the website list upon each reprint.

Index

A
Agriculture 27
  barley 34
  beef 35
  cattle 34
  chicken 34
  eggs 34
  fish 34
  milk 34, 35
  pork 34, 35
  rice 34
  root crops 34
  vegetables 34
Asian Games 54

B
Beomeosa temple 74
Boseong, South Jeolla province 34
Buddha's Birthday 86
Bukchon Hanok Village 56
Bulguksa temples 55
Bupheong District 67
Busan 28, 39, 71, 74
Busan Cinema Center 57
Buses 39

C
Changdeokgung Palace 30
Changnyeong temple 59
Children's Day 86
Chinese
  Cantonese 47
  Mandarin 47
Choson Dynasty 8, 19, 20, 22, 48, 49, 58, 63, 68, 69
  Annals of 20
Chung-hee, Park 23
Chuseok 86
Computer services 35
Confucian classics 62

D
Dae-jung, Kim 24
Daegu 38, 70
  Otgol Village 72
Daejeon 38
Daewoo 37
danji buildings 55
Demilitarized Zone 22, 65
Democratic People's Republic of Korea (DPRK) 22
Deogyusan National Park 10
Dol hareubangs, statues 18
Dongdaemun Design Plaza 57
Doo-hwan, Chun 23

E
E-World Daegu. 71
Economic problems 42
Education 50

F
Festivals and holidays 86
FIFA World Cup 52, 53
Filipinos 45

Flag of South Korea 8
Floating Islands 57
Flora and Fauna
  bears 15
  camellia japonica 16
  Demilitarized Zone 16
  Eurasian lynx 15, 17
  Korean pines 16
  Siberian tiger 15
Food and drink
  andong Soju 48
  bibimbap 82, 83
  kimchi 84
  munbaeju 48
  sanseong Soju 48

G
Ganghwa dolmens 19
Ganghwado Island 87
Gangwon 12
Geun-hye, Park 24
Goguryeo tombs 58
Golden Age of Painting 58
Goryeo Dynasty 22
Gross Domestic Product (GDP) 27, 29, 30, 33, 34, 35, 77, 78, 80
Gwangandaegyo Bridge 73
Gwangji 38
Gyeonggi province 11, 67, 68
Gyeongsabgbuk-do province 10, 70

H

Hadid, Zaha 57
Haeundae Beach 28
Hanbok traditional costume 44
Hangeul Day 86, 87
Hanok villages 56
Himmelblau, Coop 57
Hirohito, Emperor of Japan 24
Hwarangdo 62
Hwaseong fortress 69
Hyundai 30, 37
Hyundai Heavy Industries 37

I

Imports and Exports 30
Incheon 12, 39, 66
Independence Movement Day 86
Industrial sector 36
Industries
  automobile production 27, 33
  chemicals 27, 33
  electronics 33
  shipbuilding 27, 33
  steel 27, 33
  telecommunications 27, 33

J

Jae-in, Moon 24
Japan 24
Japanese 46
Jeju City 13, 28
Jeju Folklore & Natural History Museum 28
Jeju Island 12, 13, 18
  province 28
Jeollabuk-do province 10
Jeonju Hanok Village 60
Jong-il, Kim 24
Jong-un, Kim 24
Jongmyo temple 66

K

K-drama 79
K-pop 61, 62, 79
Kennedy, John F. 23
Kia 37
King Taejo 20
Kite flying 51, 53
Korail passes 41
Korea Annexation Treaty 24
Korea
  diaspora 45
  Strait 11
  Train Express 40
Korean
  peninsula 7
  Wave 62
  Americans 45
  Chinese 45
Kory-saram 45

L

Labor force 32
Lantern Festival 87
Liberation Day 86
Liberty Park 67

M

Memorial Day 86
Mi-rae, Yoon 61
Ministry of Culture 79
Minwha painting 58
Mount
  Hallasan 7, 13, 28
  Manisan 87
Mr. Sunshine in Daegu 70
Mugunghwa train 40

N

N. Seoul Tower 28
Nakdong River 12
Namsan Park 28
National Foundation Day 86
National Opera Group 62
Nepalese 46
New Year's Day 86
Nobel Peace Prize 24
North Korea 7, 11

O

Okpo, Geoje 36

P

Ports
  Busan 38, 72
  Gunsan 38
  Incheon 38
  Kwangyang 38
  Mokpo 38
  Pohang 38
  Ulsan 38
  Yeosu 38

93

Presidents Cup 54
Pyolgok poetry 62

R
Religion
  Buddhism 48
   Won 49
  Cheondogyo 49
  Christianity 48
  Confucianism 22, 48, 58
  Daejonggyo 49
  shamanism 48
  Won Buddhism 49
Renault 37
Republic of Korea (ROK) Armed Forces 52
Retail shopping 35
Russians 46

S
Saemaeul services 40
Samsung 32
  Heavy Industries 37
Sea of Japan 7, 11
Seokjeon Daeje ceremony 60
Seollal 86
Seorak-san 15
Seoul 28, 39, 40, 56, 57, 64, 65, 71
  station 21, 41
shamanistic music 60
South Korean subway 38
Sri Lankans 46

Ssireum 54
Standard Korean language 46
STX Europe 37
Summer Olympic Games, Seoul 23, 54
Summer World Military Games 54
Suwon 68

T
T-Money card 38
Tae kwon do 54
Tae-woo, Roh 23
Taejongdae park 74
Taiwanese 46
Tha 46
Tiger JK 61
Tourism 28
Tourism Help Line 39
Transportation 37

U
UNESCO World Heritage Site 30
Unified Silla Dynasty 62

W
Winter Olympic Games 25
Won (Currency) 30
World Baseball Classic 53

Y
Yellow Sea 7
Yeongdo Lighthouse 74
Yeonpo Galbi 69
Yin-and-yang 8
Yongin Everline Metropolitan Subway (AGT) 38
Young-sam, Kim 24

Organizations to Contact

For general inquiries into traveling in South Korea and for brochure requests, contact:

STA Travel

722 Broadway, New York NY 10003.

Phone: (212) 473-6100

Toll Free: 800-781-4040

Website: www.statravel.com

Korea Tourism Organization Headquarters

10, Segye-ro, Wonju-si, Gangwon-do. 26464

Repubic of Korea

Phone: +82-33-738-3000

Website: http://english.visitkorea.or.kr/enu/index.kto

Tripsavvy

1500 Broadway, New York, NY 10036.

Phone: (212) 204-4000

Website: https://www.tripsavvy.com/travel-to-south-korea-1458487

U.S. Embassy Seoul, South Korea

188 Sejong-daero, Jongno-gu,

Seoul, Korea 03141

Phone: +82-2-397-4114

Website: https://kr.usembassy.gov

Author's Biography

Catrina Daniels-Cowart is a freelance writer and educator, travel enthusiast, and author of children's books. Her passion for travel around the world began with an interest in international fashions, medical technology, and cultural inclusion. Today, she teaches English as a second language and documents unique differences between the cultures she encounters. She currently lives in Kentucky with her husband, two dogs, and neighborhood cat.

Picture Credits

All images in this book are in the public domain or have been supplied under license by © Shutterstock.com. Page 1 Maxim Tupikov, pages 2-3 Kenneth Deden, page 8 Daboost, page 9 Tungchenng, page 10 Guitar photographer, page 13 Nattee Chalermtiragool, page 17 Stanislav Duben, page 18 Noppasin Wongchum, page 19 Takashi Images, page 21 ST_Travel, page 26 Mnimage, page 28 Sarin Kunthong, page 29 One_Clear_Vision, page 31 Sorbis, page 32 Paulsat, page 34 ST_Travel, page 35 Sorbis, page 36 BNK Maritime Photographer, page 37 Hyundai, page 38 Maxim Tupikov, page 40 2p2play, page 41 EQRoy, page 42 TZIDOSUN, page 43 Niyazz, page 44 Charlie, Waradee, page 45 KPG_Mega, page 46 Elwynn, page 49 Joshua Davenport, page 50 Imtmphoto, page 52 Yuri Gurevich, page 53 Panwasin Seemala, page 54 Yeongsik Im, page 55 twoKim images, page 56 CJ Naltanani, page 59 TamasV, page 60 Yeonsik Im, page 54 Guitar photographer, page 66 Lukas Bischoff Photography, page 68 redstart, page 69 FenlioQ, page 71 Njhia Khanh, page 72 Mali Lucky, page 73 Sean Pavone, page 74 Artyooran, page 75 Agnieszka Skalska, page 76 Panwasin Seemala, page 78 Natthawat Utsawachaichot, page 80 KPG/Vary. Page 61 Wikimedia Commons/LG

Front cover: © ESB Professional; CJ Nattana; StephanScherhag; Noppasin Wongchuml

To the best knowledge of the publisher, all images not specifically credited are in the public domain. If any image has been inadvertently uncredited, please notify the publisher, so that credit can be given in future printings.

Video Credits

Page 14: Geography Now, http://x-qr.net/1JQf
Page 20: This is Korea, http://x-qr.net/1LL5
Page 37: ARIRANG NEWS, http://x-qr.net/1Lxh
Page 51: CNN, http://x-qr.net/1Kyt
Page 67: Uneed2know, http://x-qr.net/1M2Y